LUMP

19 Monologues from a 27-Year-Old Breast Cancer Survivor

Leena Luther

LUMP

Copyright © 2011 Sublimity Press

All rights reserved. No part of this book may be reproduced, stored in a retrieval system, or transmitted in any form or by means, without the prior written permission of the publisher, except in the case of brief quotations embedded in critical articles or reviews.

Neither the author, Sublimity Press, nor its dealers or distributers will be held liable for any damages caused or alleged to be caused directly or indirectly by this book.

Sublimity Press has endeavored to provide trademark information about all the companies and products mentioned in this book by appropriate use of capitals. However, Sublimity Press cannot guarantee the accuracy of this information.

First published: June 2011

ISBN-13: 978-0615484501
LCCN: 2011909392

www.sublimitypress.com
www.leenaluther.com

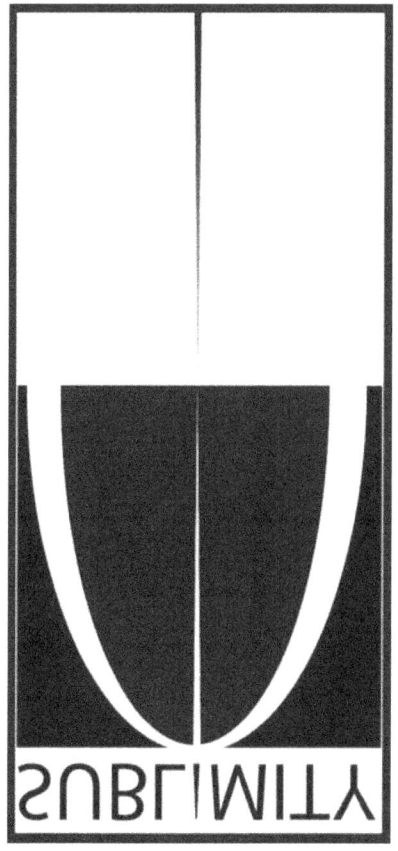

Sublimity Press

LUMP

Table of Contents

Table of Contents iii
Introduction v

Him 1
I Love New York 5
Skeptical Looks 9
The Princess with the Pea 15
Odds Are 17
Checking Out the Goods in the Chemo Room 21
Soap Opera Fantasy Land 27
Why Bloodhounds Look So Sad 31
Whipping Off the Wig 33
Chemo Dreams 39
The Power of Puff 43
My Orange Tic Tac 47
Mistaken Identity 53
My Cat Plays the Harp, and Other Non Sequiturs 57
Scars 63
Dress Code 67
The Fourth State of Matter 71
The Crone Goddess-in-Training Definition
of a Hot Flash 75
The 5th Annual "Leena's Not Dead" Party 81

Young People and Breast Cancer 85
Author Assessments 89
Performance Rights 91
Acknowledgements 93
Giving Back 95
Performance Notes 97

Introduction

Let me choose my words carefully, here. Breast cancer is something that happened to me.

There were no risk factors. I was 27 years old, had no family history of breast cancer, and I exercised regularly. It happened anyway.

Huh. Weird.

I never felt particularly brave or tragic or strong or hurt by the breast cancer. I don't think I was flippant, either. It's a hard thing to explain to people. So I wrote this book to show them.

These monologues are arranged chronologically, more or less, for those who wish to read it as a narrative. But I encourage readers to embrace the performance aspect of the work.

Each monologue lists an approximate performance length, and they range from 1 to 3 minutes long. Some are dramatic and some are comedic, but the majority encompass both traits (depending on how you interpret them). And I encourage performers to interpret the monologues in crazy ways.

This was my life. Enjoy!

—Leena

Him
2 Minutes

He made the exchange; biting hard on my nipple for a slap in the face. He knew I hated that, so it hurt me in more ways than one.

I pulled myself back to the edges of his knees, my hands forming a barrier as I tried to rub the pain away. My left breast, in particular, was very sore. And of course he had picked that one, so I now had pain radiating twice.

He was sorry. He had gotten carried away. He was caught up in the moment. Hadn't he always behaved himself before? He had, and I forgave him, though I still pouted a bit.

I found the lump a few days later, lying in his bed. I thought it was a lump anyway. The pain still radiated and I was growing desperate to find its source. I asked him for a second opinion. Yes, he could feel that. It felt like the knots in my back. The groping soon turned sexual, so our conversation turned to other things.

He left for work and I left for another day of job hunting, but I called my mother from his driveway. We didn't have any history of breast cancer, did we? No, I didn't think so. Yes Mom. I'll find a doctor.

The doctor found a mammogram machine, an ultrasound, and a biopsy.

He didn't want a girlfriend anymore. He couldn't do it: the nurturing, the respect, the thinking of anyone besides himself. I said he needed a warning tattooed on his forehead. Yes, he agreed. Unlucky women fell for him all the time. I couldn't stop crying. It was too bad for me, but excellent for his fuck friends. As I cried at home, he flew one of them in for the week. I think it was "Baltimore." She called a lot, but perhaps one of the others.

He prided himself on discretion, so he discreetly went home everyday at lunch to chomp on her nipples, which meant discreetly shifting his behavior back to what was so recognizable before I came along. He was discreet enough that everyone in his office knew exactly what he was doing. They discreetly warned me.

The news was hard to get. The doctor had found the cancer.

I Love New York
2 ½ Minutes

Some information should only be conveyed in slogan form, don't you think? Little ditties. Soundbites. Short, straightforward statements. This lets the maximum number of people understand what's going on. Some may say it hits the "lowest common denominator."

Does that insult your intelligence?

I said "sometimes," not "all the time." Just those times when your brain goes all numb and your bloodstream electrifies and your reasoning capabilities turn to mush. You need a slogan, just to get by for a little bit.

Not convinced? Fine. What if I told you the Buddhists have been doing it since the eleventh century? "In all activities, train with slogans." That's one of their slogans. They don't even wait until they are freaking out. They use them all the time. So there.

It was a weird phone call, as you might expect, the phone call that told me I had cancer.

She didn't use a straightforward statement, not really. It was more like a riddle. "You have breast cancer. But don't worry. It's not the bad kind," she told me.

"Umm… 'kay." "Don't ponder others," the Buddhists say.

She then told me that Colorado had a few programs that could help me out financially. But I needed to come in and fill out the paperwork right away.

"Oh, that's okay," I said. "I'll be in New York."

Now it was her turn to be confused. "New York?"

"Yeah, I'm moving to New York." "I Love NY." Everybody knows that one.

"Do you really think that's a good idea?" she asked.

"Of course!" Why she was so resistant to the idea? Take a tip from the Buddhists and, "Don't malign others," lady.

But there was another awkward silence, followed by a delicately-worded lecture on how moving was stressful. And cancer was stressful. And didn't I want to be home?

I laughed. I suddenly understood the slogan that must have been running through her head.
"If I can make it there, I'll make it anywhere!"

So, okay, fine. Maybe slogans aren't for everyone. I got my brain out of the numbness and my bloodstream un-electrified enough to explain.

"I'm from New York. Upstate. I moved to Colorado a few years ago, and it hasn't really worked out for me. New York is my home. All my support is there. My family is there. I recognize that this time will be difficult. I'm going back."

And then I thanked her. Because, as the Buddhists teach, "Be grateful to everyone."

Skeptical Looks
3 Minutes

"You're going to gain weight," my doctor told me.

I looked at him like he was out of his mind. I gave doctors that look a lot, actually, in the beginning. But they kept telling me weird things. Things in official-sounding voices. Things like, "You have cancer. But not the bad kind."

Or, "The main tumor we removed now tests benign. We must have sucked out all the cancerous parts in the biopsy. Remember that big needle?"

How about, "It did spread to your lymph nodes though. That means you get chemo, which is actually good.

You're young and strong enough for aggressive treatment, so why not?"

And now, "You're going to gain weight on chemotherapy."

I'm a naturally skeptical person, and I certainly don't believe everything I see on TV. But aren't folks on chemo supposed to be throwing up all the time? Weak and skinny?

"You see, some patients have bad allergic reactions to some of the drug cocktails. But, we can generally prevent that with the administration of steroids. You'll not only have the munchies, you'll feel so jittery that you'll be cleaning your closet at three in the morning."

I gave him that skeptical look again, but, whatever. What is all this talk of weight gain and closets anyway? It's like I entered a chick-lit novel. A chick-lit novel narrated by an official-sounding voice. Weird.

I just hoped it meant my prognosis was so awesome that this silly stuff was all we needed to talk about. I could kiss my size four body goodbye if it meant I got to keep it a good, long time.

That's not how it works. I didn't get to take a time out from my life and the things I cared about. Cancer didn't change that. I was still a 20-something trying to figure out her life. I was still heartbroken over a failed relationship. I wanted a good job. I wanted to stay pretty. And definitely to keep my young person metabolism! You know, to comfort myself with half a gallon of ice cream, yet still look good in my jeans.

It's like the doctor knew, that a year and a half later, I'd be selling all my pre-cancer clothes at a garage sale. That I would be as cured as possible, but still crying.

I kept waiting for it. That complete shift in perspective. But it never came. Not really. Maybe I'm a bad cancer patient for admitting that. For admitting that I spent more time stressing about my love life than my illness. For not sucking up the weight gain, or the year I didn't work, or the fact that I had to raid my 401K to get by. Those things weren't some cancer badge of honor. They sucked. I hated those things. I hated them so much.

And that's the thing. They could have happened to me anyway. Maybe they would have. They could have happened to any 27-year-old girl. It wasn't cancer's fault.

Are you looking at me skeptically now? I can see that you are.

I don't mean to say that it didn't matter. That it didn't count. That I wasn't scared, or didn't remember every day that I was sick.

Just, I didn't experience any of the narratives that were never mine to start with. You know, the cancer stories. I didn't lose faith. I didn't find God. I didn't win the Tour de France. I just didn't.

I may have been 27, and trying to figure myself out. But, it turns out I was me all along. Cancer didn't form me. It didn't create me. I didn't rise from its ashes.

I was still me, just with cancer.

The Princess with the Pea
1 ½ Minutes

It feels like the princess was right to lose sleep over a pea. It may be small, but it's not supposed to be there.

Wouldn't it be funny, if this were all some sort of princess test? I can see the updated version now. It would be some Fox- or MTV-inspired reality show. Nine ladies, one pea. *Who* is the biggest princess? In a surprising twist, the pea is revealed to be a cancerous tumor. AHHHH! Watch them all scream.

I think I may be acting more troll than princess though. Ask my family, they'll tell you I grunt a lot. And my cats won't leave my side, like little minions. Or is that more princessy? Minions seem like something they should have too. And a dashing prince. I did go on a date last night, mostly to prove to myself that I still could. He was tall. He did have dark hair. And he did kiss me.

He was just being gallant though. He left to go on vacation to a far-away land, and I, the fair maiden he so chivalrously distracted, have an adventure of my own this morning. Surgery, the start of many adventures coming my way. I'm laying here in rags on an uncomfortable bed, waiting for them to put me under.

Heh. Waiting for the princess with the pea to turn into a sleeping beauty.

Odds Are
2 Minutes

I'm scared to go on a plane because there is a one in ten million chance of the plane crashing. Not to mention the one in 30 million chance of losing cabin pressure.

Think about it. How many people fly each day? I don't even know, but it's pretty likely that these stats don't take that variable into account. I got them off the internet. But if each person flying has a one in ten million chance of going down, then, before too long, someone is doomed. Once a month, at least.

Is that fuzzy math? I never enjoyed probability. I never enjoyed heights either. I can actually quantify how much. If I go above 15 stories, my legs die on me. My arms work okay though, and they pull me along the ground towards the nearest elevator. Seriously. Ask my seventh grade classmates about our trip to the World Trade Center. That was last time I tried to be brave about heights.

So, okay, I concur that the fear of heights thing crystallizes the whole flying-odds thing into freaky shapes in my brain. Stabby little shapes, those are. But other things scare me too, like taking new medicines.

It's because of all those side effects you hear about in the commercials. I wish those commercials were illegal. No one needs to hear about that. Especially sick people. I don't even get those effects, actually. I get the ones that are too rare to require lawful advertisement mentions. I start a new medicine and something bizarre happens. It always ends with a call to a skeptical pharmacist who has to look it up, and then eat it.

I shouldn't have been surprised about the lump, honestly. My body is so weird.

But the odds of getting a lump are pretty good. If you have boobs, at some point, there'll be a lump in there. And that's fine. That's honestly nothing to be afraid of. Because the odds, the on-the-ground odds, say it's just density, or a cyst, or even a benign tumor.

There was less than half a percent, I was told, of the lump being cancerous, given my young age and complete lack of family history. But there it was. A cancerous lump in my chest, and more in my lymph nodes, it turned out.

So now I feel like I'm on the top of the Burj Khalifa, and no one will let me off. There is an elevator, but it'll take me ten years to reach it. That's what the doctors say. I'm also told I'll crawl faster as the years pass, but the first few will be excruciatingly slow.

So please pardon me if I don't want to fly. Or when I hesitate to swallow a new pill. Or the failure of a hundred other anxiety-induced challenges. I know I'm being ridiculous. I hate it as much as you do. I just don't know the odds that I'll ever get over this.

Checking Out the Goods in the Chemo Room
3 Minutes

You don't get your own private spot to get poisoned. No. It's you and a bunch of others, all getting poisoned at the same time. There are various green chairs set up around the room, so you can stare at each other. Smaller, less comfy chairs surround the green ones, so loved ones can get in on the fun. Only two loved ones per green chair though. Any more would be too crowded.

It wasn't any nicer than a typical hospital room. No cheerful colors or good lighting or rugs. No TV either. The walls were decorated with warning signs, telling the loved ones to lay off the cologne and smelly lotion, and telling us victims to get our ports flushed regularly to prevent blood clots and death.

Despite their best intentions, I could still smell all the rubber from their medical tubes. The scent of the iodine and alcohol slathered over my port permeated my nose with ease. It was gross.

The port itself, well, that was a good time. They fused a plastic disk directly into one of the big veins in my chest. It lived under my skin, giving me a big bump that freaked people out if they noticed it. But it was better to get the poison through the port than through your arm. Chemo was harsh and shredded the wimpy arm veins to bits.

So every two weeks, I sat in my green chair of choice and got poison plugged into my chest. My mom, usually, sat next to me and read a book. I tried to read too, but more often than not I found myself staring off into space, half noticing things about the others in the room. That one looks old. That one looks older. That one looks dead already. Wait a sec., *that one looks hot!*

I developed a crush on a fellow poison victim. He seemed my age, or at least somewhere in his 20s. He had a nice, even face, with full lips and ears that stuck out a bit. I'm a sucker for ears that stick out a bit. His hair was dark, buzzed short and molting like mine, except he wore no hat. An older man and a woman sat protectively around his green chair. *Yes! Maybe that meant he was single.* I couldn't tell what color his eyes were, because they were closed, but any color would have looked good. His face kept grimacing. Clearly, he wasn't having a good time. His parents didn't notice me staring at him. My mom didn't notice either. So I continued.

I felt for this kid and wondered what kind of cancer he had. Was it one of the easier ones? Or was he pretty much doomed? He was too young for this, as was I. I watched him struggle with his misery and longed to alleviate it, just a little bit. I wanted to smile at him. Not the "sympathetic" sort, or the "this totally sucks" sort, but the full on "Hey, I think you are awesome" sort of smile that would completely make him forget where he was as he was jolted into a reality where some mysterious hot woman with piercing blue eyes was checking him out.

And then I remembered I wasn't exactly mysterious, sitting in my green chair with poison stuck in me. I looked down at my chest. My hotness factor was pretty weak too, even though my blue hat did bring out my eyes. The half-missing eyebrows framing them were hard to miss. I shuddered because I was cold and slumped because I was weak. This was a situation he knew all too well, and there was nothing attractive about it.

I looked up again and noticed he was sleeping. So I closed my eyes and slept too.

Soap Opera Fantasy Land
2 ½ Minutes

Nana introduced me to her "stories" when I was quite young. I'd stay at her house for a week or two each summer, learning all the ins and outs of Pine Valley, Llanview, and Port Charles. Those are the settings of soap operas, for those of you not in the know.

Both the likeliest and the unlikeliest things happened on these shows. On the likely end of things, people got cheated on, characters turned to substance abuse, and babies were born. These ordinary things had to occur, to make the shows relatable.

The real entertainment lay in the unlikely things. The wonder of daytime shone in people coming back from the dead, aliens and vampires, and the fact that people could be brilliant scientists, lawyers, and bounty hunters, all at the same time. For years, I casually enjoyed these crazy antics. I didn't watch every day, but I certainly kept up, once a week or so.

Then one day my soaps stunned me. An event occurred that was both likely and unlikely to me. Young Emily Quartermaine was diagnosed with breast cancer.

At the same time I was.

Now, I'm the first to gleefully admit that every single one of my names (first, last, and the two middle) appear on various soap operas. That's funny. But the Emily/cancer parallel freaked me out. I suddenly saw myself up there, a 20-something with breast cancer. How on Earth did I find myself in the middle of one of these crazy soap opera situations?

It was highly bizarre, getting breast cancer a mere 15 years after you first got breasts. Yet, in mine and Emily's cases, it was as real as it got.

So, of course, I handled it like any soap opera character would. I started writing threatening letters to the people in charge.

Dear Bob Guza,

I will kill you, you know, if you kill off Emily. I've checked various reliable online sources, and I see no indication that the actress's contract is ending, so I consider this a good sign. However, don't you dare kill her off from cancer and bring her back as an evil twin. Or you'll be sorry.

P.S.—Real patients aren't allowed to wear make-up to surgery. Painted nails are also a no no, as the polish interferes with the machines ability to calculate your pulse. The pulse you won't have if you kill Emily. FYI.

P.P.S.—I like what you did using real breast cancer support groups on the show. That was nice. I hope you reassured the actual patients that Emily wasn't going to die. If not, I'm sure I can recruit some help for my hit squad.

It was all very dramatic. But since no one came to arrest me, not too dramatic, I guess. Death threats must be both likely and unlikely in their world. It must have taught them to cope.

Why Bloodhounds Look So Sad
1 Minute

I'm making people paranoid. They walk by and I cringe. My head turns away and my face scrunches up like I've just smelled an exceptionally pissy skunk that's been wading in a kiddie pool full of compost. Or, you know, some other smell that defines the word putrid.

Because I have.

That's not to say you all stink. You might, but unless you've been walking said skunk, you're probably fine. I can't tell the difference anymore. My sense of smell is like a superpower.

Yay chemo.

I'm not sure how it works exactly. I know that the drugs are killing off all the fast-growing cells in my body, like the tumor, my hair, my stomach lining, and evidently that lovely cushion that lives in my nasal passages and acts like a shield so I don't have to know what's in my neighbor's garbage.

Or armpit.

I think that's why bloodhounds look so sad, actually, because we still have cancer patients around, putting their own keen sense of smell to shame. Let's work on a cure, shall we? For the animals.

Whipping Off the Wig
3 Minutes

My mom was ready to make a ruckus.

"Excuse me. I think you're in our seats." My grandmother, mother, and I peered at the little old ladies in row G of the High School auditorium. After a few moments of fruitless staring, I decided to be helpful and showed them my ticket. Grandma merely beamed in little old lady solidarity, with a dose of Alzheimer's. "Hello. My grandson is a police officer."

I don't know if they actually expected us to call the police, but they moved, giving us dirty looks the whole time. *Hmmph*, their expressions said. We are *old*. We can't *see* the stage unless we sit *right here*. How dare they ask us to *move*.

They made their way to their crappy seats. I couldn't blame them for trying to upgrade, but their combined evil eye was intense and started to make me mad. So, I whipped off my wig and yelled, "Having cancer trumps being old, so there!"

Okay, so I didn't really say that, but I wanted to. I thought it would be funny.

My bald head has been the source of much hilarity, and grief. Before the cancer, I had long, thick hair, untouched by perms or dye. It was unbroken, pure, and fucking gorgeous, if I do say so myself. I didn't want to see it go, but since the alternative was, well, death, I decided to be a good sport about it.

I cut it off in stages. The first step was a shoulder-length haircut, with layers. "Are you going to style it?" the hairdresser asked anxiously. "Because I don't think we should cut layers unless you plan on curling it. It's too straight." My hair fell from her scissors onto my chest, covering up my chemo port. "Sure," I answered, knowing that in two weeks the whole thing would be moot.

The second step was bangs. I hadn't had bangs since an unfortunate self-attempt in high school. But unless you wanted to spend a zillion dollars on a Hollywood-quality wig, spirit gum, and stage makeup, you ended up with bangs to hide the wig line. I didn't have a zillion dollars, so I thought I should try and get used to it.

The third step was a mohawk. That was the plan anyway. I told my friend Cheryl all about it, gleeful and excited. She laughed and advised me to do it before my next treatment, because the chemo made me feel like crap and I wouldn't be so cheerful. She was right, but I didn't listen to her. The mohawk attempt concluded with odd chunks of my head shaved, the clippers thrown against the wall, and me throwing up and sobbing.

But, like I said, it was all moot soon enough. That Christmas I sat next to my police officer brother for dinner, our heads matching and gleaming. Our sister found this very amusing, and giggled as she looked back and forth between the two of us. "Watch it," I said. "You're next if you keep that up." But I laughed too. It was funny.

My bald head was actually useful to people. I visited Cheryl, and her roommate's son wouldn't brush his hair. She whispered to him, "Leena wouldn't brush her hair either. Do you know what happened then? Do you know what we did to her?" He shook his head, eyes wide, not expecting Cheryl to whip my wig off. He screamed. That was funny too.

Oh, my bald head, reducing me to laughing at old women and little boys. That was never the plan, but, sometimes you have to go with what life sets out for you.

Chemo Dreams
2 Minutes

A spiny, little hedgehog thing was following my friends around. It was brown and thorny. It had no face. It had no features. It had no ears. I wasn't even sure it was alive. And I hated it.

    I tried to kill it. I wanted it dead and gone. I beat it with a baseball bat.

    It squealed, but wouldn't die.

    My friends just watched me.

    I wanted it gone, especially after I failed to kill it. It was mocking me with its presence. It seemed more alive because it would not die.

I tried and tried and tried to kill it.

Of course, this was a cancer dream. One of the more obvious ones, not that that made it any less terrifying.

Most of my dreams are violent and gruesome these days. Is it the chemo? The radiation? The fact that I have fucking cancer? I don't know.

Even when they start out nice, something happens in them that reminds me of cancer. Like, a man appears who looks just like the parking attendant at the hospital. Or I'll be resting in the sand by the side of a road. I lay down and tried to take a nap, but ants keep going into the track marks in my arm and taking little grains of sand away.

But usually it's something gross, and everyone ends up beating the shit out of each other. Everyone is bloody.

Everyone can barely crawl. Everyone is a big mess, and sick of fighting.

Whatever, I tell myself. Some people have fucked up dreams anyway. That's what dreams are. They aren't real. I long for that, a fucked-up dream that bears no relation to what's going on in my life. When did I become so damn Freudian? I was pretty well-adjusted about all this, I thought. But then I go to bed and I'm not so sure.

Because that's when I make a little girl eat her dead relatives, because it's her only hope of staying alive. I pluck every hair off of my face. I paint my breasts red so everyone can see them. I drink poison, over and over, because it will save me, but I still end up dead.

The Power of Puff
2 Minutes

I don't believe in a lot of things. I don't believe in six impossible things before breakfast. I don't believe a fairy godmother will come solve all my problems. And I don't believe that being cheerful will make my cancer go away.

Please don't misunderstand. I don't suffer from a lack of imagination. I just keep it in its place. I think Alice in Wonderland is a great book. I have a few more issues with Cinderella, but, it's still fun. And I like being cheerful. It helps pass the time more pleasantly.

They hadn't taken the tumor out yet, you see. It was like a ticking time bomb in my chest. I can't even tell you how much I just wanted it out. But I had to wait three weeks until surgery. What the fuck? I had to do something, right?

So I did a visualization exercise.

I'm not exactly sure what a tumor looks like, inside the body. I don't really want to know. There will be no Google image searches for my benefit.

Nope, cartoons. Cartoons will do the trick!

I decided to ramp up the creativity and use a cartoon I've never even seen, about three kindergarten girls with superpowers—The Powerpuff Girls. That's all I needed to know. Kindergartners scare me a bit. They're way too little to know so much. And they learn it so fast. Add in some superpowers? Yes! Those are some awesome allies.

Off they went, thousands of Blossoms, Bubbles, and Buttercups, patrolling my body with their big eyes and big heads. If they came across some cell gone awry, they kicked its ass. And the big tumor? They pummeled that one daily.

It helped pass the time anyway.

When I woke up from surgery, I was told something odd. The tumor was now non-cancerous, as in; they could find no cancerous cells on the main tumor.

Wow. Did the Powerpuff girls save me?

Not quite. The cancer had spread to my lymph nodes, so, I had it alright. Since the tumor was small to start with, they reasoned that all the cancerous cells were removed during the core biopsy, which is a fancy name for really thick needle.

I buy that explanation, honestly. Stranger things have happened.

But that didn't stop me from using the girls again during chemotherapy. And radiation. Maybe each one took the lead in a different part. Maybe. I don't believe it, but I like to think it. Like I said, it helps pass the time.

My Orange Tic Tac
3 Minutes

My orange Tic Tac is serious.

It's also my stock answer for one of the silliest questions in the world, "What's your most prized possession?"

"My orange Tic Tac."

It sounds like I'm making a joke, doesn't it?

A friend of mine gave it to me in high school. "Wanna Tic Tac?" she asked me. "Sure," I replied. But then I realized she was holding a pack of the orange, nasty-tasting ones. "Oh, never mind," I told her. "I don't like that kind."

That's when she started giving me a hard time. She was good at that. She was good at everything. She was smarter and more creative. She wrote better, and even had prettier eyes. But that was okay. She didn't feel superior, not to me anyway. I was smart and creative, wrote well and had pretty eyes too.

I was in on the joke.

"Fine," she said. "If my Tic Tacs aren't good enough for you…"

I caved after about 30 seconds of teasing, which is pathetic. She deserved a better fight that that, so I raised the stakes. I told my friend that not only would I take a nasty-ass orange Tic Tac, but that I would keep it forever. Forever! Ha HA!

And as far as she was concerned, I did. Her forever only lasted five more years. Leukemia. Age 23.

I was sad, of course, even though we had grown apart after High School and the extent of our contact was running into each other at the movies that one time. I displayed all the typical laments: so tragic, too soon, her poor family, how awful.

The Tic Tac joke seemed sick at that point. It looked sick too. It sat in a tiny jewelry box, no longer orange, but a stark white. The whole thing was a grotesque science experiment, and made people uncomfortable when I showed it to them.

But soon enough, that discomfort comforted me. It was like we were joking around again. On the outside, it may seem a little messed up, but we knew better. I decided to keep it then, for my forever. It was a last hurrah. She wasn't the only one who could raise the bar. Tic Tac, tit-for-tat, my forever, take that!

Four years later, I was diagnosed too. Breast cancer. Age 27.

The Tic Tac had turned grey. Any pretense of a shiny finish was gone.

I imagined all sorts of things. I imagined our pretty eyes without eyelashes. I imagined our intelligence blunted by medicine. I imagined our creativity sleeping, and waiting for a better time to come out. I imagined once beautiful music failing to comfort the brutal thought of death. I imagined the end of her forever. And I imagined the end of mine.

But then I got better. I didn't put up a better fight. I just happened to get better. My eyelashes came back. So did my intelligence and creativity. All music became beautiful again—life-affirming and beautiful, like laughter.

I just checked the Tic Tac the other day. It's a deep brown now. It's even kinda shiny again. Weird, how that works. I know someday, it will change again. And someday, I will reach my forever. I hope I can look at my orange Tic Tac and laugh.

Mistaken Identity
1 ½ Minutes

Sometimes I forget I have cancer. It's quite easy, sometimes, to put my other identities first and foremost. Even in the oncology waiting room.

I saw a guy there—someone I had gone to High School with ten years ago. My first though was, "Wow, he's balding," the irony completely lost on me. I just wanted to say hi, because I was one of those kids that actually enjoyed High School. At that time, I was oblivious to most of the awkwardness that actually mattered to anyone. I was a little socially inept that way. But it worked for me, because I was also quiet. So instead of blurting out the first thing that came into my head, I usually said something witty like, "Oh… okay." No harm done.

That's what it was like in the oncology waiting room. I politely waited until the man seated next to him was called away. His father, evidently. The greeting was still awkward, but it could have been worse. He took it like a pro—a cancer waiting room professional.

My mother often came with me to my appointments. I can't even tell you the number of times other waiting room folk told me, "It's so nice of you to come be here with your mom during this difficult time."

I'd want to blurt out, "Damn, this wig is good. Mom, maybe you need a haircut."

No one else would have found that funny though. Especially not my mom (for the record, she has very nice hair).

We were constantly confusing people. How do you answer that? It seemed rude either way. I can't take the credit that my mother so richly deserves. And I shouldn't go around telling strangers how wrong they are. But I had to choose.

"She's actually here for me."

Cancer is always putting me in these situations. It's worse than High School.

"Hey! Your walk shirt is pink! I love it! I want one."

"No, you don't."

"How did you get it?"

"I had cancer."

"Oh… okay."

Don't worry. No harm done.

My Cat Plays the Harp, and Other Non Sequiturs
3 Minutes

For the longest time, I didn't know what non sequitur meant. I usually look these things up straight away. I don't like not knowing things. But it sounds so snooty, doesn't it? *Non sequitur.* I was never interested in being snooty.

Smart, though, smart is important. I'm actually smart enough to be in Mensa. My test scores say so. But, really, how do you join the high IQ society? The society that says you are smarter than anyone else around? How do you do that without being snooty? How do you even tell people that without being snooty?

I guess I'm being snooty. Excuse me. I've been lying in bed a very long time.

Right there, that makes me terribly uninteresting. I'm not doing anything fun in bed, like sex or having whacked out dreams. I'm just lying here, being boring. And turning into a moron.

Well, I am recovering from chemotherapy. I guess that makes me tragic, to some. But trust me. It's mostly boring. I don't think I'm supposed to talk about it like that though.

Not that anyone expects me to be witty.

They tell me about this thing called "chemo brain." Basically, that chemo not only makes you feel like you were run over by a truck for a few days, it makes your brain all foggy and forgetful too.

It may or may not be true. But I'm not taking any chances. I don't mind pain. I don't mind fatigue. But I can't stand being stupid. I'm trying to fend it off like some people can fend off Alzheimers. My grandmother has Alzheimers. And my great-grandmother before her. I should be doing my brain exercises anyway. I have my giant book of Mensa puzzles that I take with me to chemo. Did you know that the word assassin comes from Iran? People doing murdery-type things under the influence of hashish were called hashashins. It's true. I guess we couldn't say hashashin with a straight face.

But wait, what was I talking about? Non sequiturs. It's a weird French phrase or term or label or whatever. I looked it up eventually. Despite my doing endless puzzles and math problems and vocabulary tests, non sequitur pretty much sums up what's coming out my mouth these days.

I'm totally losing my filter. And I'm starting to blurt this shit out to people. Random, unconnected, silly shit. The kind of shit that makes people go, "Ooo… kay" and scoot away at the nearest opportunity. Argh. It's lonely here in bed. I'm more impressed by minutia than ever.

And not just people I know. Strangers too, get to hear all about it. I try, with them, to share something semi-interesting, because I know it's not socially proper to pester folks with random information. I try to make the ramblings somewhat intriguing to people, but, the follow-through is a mess. Today, I discovered my cat can play the harp. Her name is Dolby. I named her after the sound system. She's aptly named. But she wasn't strumming or anything. She just plinked the strings by biting them. I just let her do it. I thought it was hilarious.

Awesome story, huh? She's probably going to snap a string. I can give her some catnip, she can break a string, and then she will known as the harp hashashin.

Sorry.

I'm going to go do a math problem now.

Scars
2 ½ Minutes

My first scar was my belly button, of course. But everyone has one, so it doesn't count. You're only special if you have an outie. Or the even more elusive innie slash outie. No such luck here.

    I used to have fun scars. The first one was when my dog bit me. Not my real dog, who was sweet as could be, but my Pound Puppy. One day as I hugged him, his hard, plastic eye scrapped my cheek. And I told anyone who would listen that Buster bit me. It made him seem less like a stuffed toy, you know? I still have him, but the scar is long gone.

I also remember the scar on my knee. I got that one from some over-zealous base running while playing kickball. In the street. You aren't really supposed to slide on gravel, you know. What a mess that was. It scarred me psychologically too. It took me years to get up the nerve to slide again. Properly, on dirt. My eventual brave attempt gave the third baseman a bloody nose in a softball game, which I got promptly kicked out of. That made me feel bad enough to cry in the dugout until someone got me a hot dog. Then it was all better.

Then came the tattoo. That counts as a scar, right? A pretty, colored scar. It didn't mean anything. I didn't want it to. I figured something I found attractive would have better staying power than something I felt was meaningful. I was self-aware enough to know that at that age, I didn't know squat. I mean, my mind was being blown at least once or twice a year. If that ever stops, I think I'll be doing something wrong. Especially since it's not that hard to blow my mind. I just told you how moved I was by a hot dog.

But then the scars stopped being fun. They weren't organic or designed. They didn't highlight my freckles or put a nifty, jagged edge along my knee.

The least noticeable is the scar on my left breast, where the main tumor was. It's about two inches long, and very thin. It's not red or puffy. It's neat and tidy. Maybe my left breast can stay sexy.

The chemo port scar is pretty ugly though. They had to open that one twice—once to slide the disk in, and once to get it out. It is red and puffy, and located right above my right breast. I think my cleavage is doomed. This is the scar I see on other folks though—that red slash across their chest that tells me they too, had cancer. Mine seems to be moving down too. That's great. My old lady bitching about gravity is going to be so much meatier than drooping complaints from the other old ladies.

Ugliest of all are the lymph node scars in my armpit. The cancer had spread there, so, out they came. The surgeon used staples to put me back together. It looked like a line accented by rows of dots. Big dots. The line is puckered, rather than puffy, because armpit skin is weird. And the indentation makes a strange shadow that makes the scar look bigger than it really is.

I don't know. Is it outside the realm of possibility that these scars will be awesome someday too? I don't think they'll fade away. But maybe they'll adorn my body like the Grand Canyon adorns the Earth.

In the meantime, I got two more tattoos, with meanings this time. One means death, or change. And the other means strength. One is all that life is going to give me, and the other is the only thing I can give life.

Dress Code
3 Minutes

The folks at the radiation center were so nice. They smiled a lot and held a general attitude that jived with mine: chemo was over now, and it was time to move onto the easy stuff. The nurses giggled and made jokes about my doctor being cute, and the doctor laughed in all the right places when I told him about my regimen of Flintstones vitamins, despite being 27 years old.

I wasn't surprised, when on the first day of actual treatment, they gave me a gift. "There's a local group that makes these for our breast cancer patients," they said, pressing the package into my hands, "Just to make your visits here a little bit nicer."

"Thank you very much," I replied, meaning it. "I'm sure it w…. Oh."

I had unwrapped a hospital gown. The frilliest, pinkest, most old lady-est hospital gown I'd ever laid eyes on.

"It's for you to keep! You can wear it every day!"

"I see. Uh. Thanks!"

Oh my GOD. I stood there in horror. There were about nine thousand flowers crammed into each square foot of fabric, each garden framed by lace that would make Queen Anne jealous. Eventually, I could see the lace hid strategically-placed Velcro, all around the torso. "That's for modesty," they whispered, greatly apologetic that I was minutes away from each and every one of them seeing my boobs. "You can keep covered up and expose only the area we need."

It was bad enough it was an ugly gift. Now it was just the *wrong* gift. I'm one of those people who rarely dress unless I have to. I'll spend whole weekends wrapped in nothing but a blanket. Nudity doesn't bother me a bit.

"I see," I said, as I looked at an old man rambling past, dressed in a faded blue hospital robe. His hiney stuck out and I was jealous.

But who was I to be ungrateful? It must have taken forever to sew on all that Velcro, and all that lace to hide the Velcro. And it even came with its own matching travel bag. Painfully, I put it on. It covered me from my voice box to the floor. I allowed myself a moment to be impressed, because I am a tall girl. If only my jeans reached down so low.

They mistook my misery for apprehension, that first day. "Just lie still. It doesn't hurt a bit. It'll be over soon."

I fled out of the hospital. When I got home, my mom asked me how it went. Wordlessly, I tossed her the travel bag, gown inside. Ten seconds later she was in stitches at the sight of the most unlikely-of-Leena garments, *ever*.

The next day, I gave the gift back. "I'm sorry," I said, "But I can't accept. It's just not... *me*. I'd feel much more comfortable if you took it back and gave it to someone who would appreciate it." Then I dressed myself in a faded, blue gown. I sauntered among the nurses, technicians, and doctors, breasts regularly exposed.

And my visits were a little bit nicer.

The Fourth State of Matter
3 Minutes

The general rule is, you heat a solid and it turns to liquid. Heat liquid, and it turns to gas. And then super hot gas, that becomes plasma. Like the sun. Four states of matter, right there. You learn it in seventh grade.

About that time, I also learned that death was coming. Do you remember the first time you realized death was coming? Not in the academic sense, but in that guttural, primal sort of way that floods your body with adrenalin. Maybe a relative died, or a pet. Or you were sitting in history class and the sheer number of dead people throughout the history of time finally hit that delicate spot in your brain.

I was listening to Warrant on my Walkman.

"Heaven isn't too far away. Closer to it every day..."

Oh fuck! It's true!

I don't think death was the message of that particular 80s hair band song, but, sometimes I can be literal. That song scared the shit out of me. Way more than my cancer diagnosis ever did.

I was right, not to be all that scared of the cancer. Here I am! The sun is shining and I'm in remission. Yes indeed. The sky is plasmastic fantastic, and I'm cancer-free.

Look at it! The rays are hitting everything—the trees, the grass, the hood of that car, my arm.

Sometimes I was scared, don't get me wrong. But my prognosis was good. My doctors were optimistic. And I could think of a lot more people that survived cancer than died from it.

I'm scared today though.

I didn't get a single panic attack during treatment. That was like, some kind of record for me. I've been having them for years. But for half a year, they stayed away. When I should have been scared, I was strong. But now, here it is.

The sun, the lovely sun, is making my arm warm. This sounds crazy, I know that. But the sun is making my skin heat up. The chemical process, it's horrible. It makes me want to cut my arm off and run away. And scream. And cry. And be anywhere but here.

I won't do any of that, of course, because that would be silly. The sun makes things warm. That's its job. I'm not hurt. I'm not in danger. The rational part of my brain keeps the nutty stuff nice and tucked in, where only I have to deal with it. That's how it works. That's how it always works.

And I know there is nothing I can do. Surgery turned into chemo. Chemo turned into radiation, and radiation turned into waiting. I'm in the fourth state of matter, just waiting to implode.

Ha. That's so trite.

What do I expect? I was the girl scared of a cheesy power ballad. Compared to that, the sun is downright terrifying.

The Crone Goddess-in-Training Definition of a Hot Flash
3 Minutes

What the hell's a hot flash?

That's the question I asked myself when told I would be taking some funky medicine to put me into medical menopause. The medicine blocked estrogen, to stop the hormone from "feeding" any breast cancer tumors. Apparently, the type of cancer I had just gotten rid of thought estrogen was yummy.

So, I'd still get my period, and all the fun that goes along with it. But I'd also get to experience the joys of menopause at age 27: hot flashes, weight gain, fatigue, mood swings. All that good stuff.

For at least five years, my doctor told me. He reserved the right to keep me on it longer. Wheeee!

I always thought I'd cherish menopause when it came. A life without cramps and ruined underwear seemed wonderful to me. Eventually. The symptoms of menopause were elusive and ignored. My 20-something mind viewed menopause as some sort of reward for a lifetime of, well, providing life. It would be like eating grapes atop Mount Olympus in gloriously white robes, without any stain remover.

Isn't that how the pagans put it? A woman past menopause is a crone, a goddess, a wise woman deserving of reverence. She has been there, done that, and looks on knowingly as us silly young folk scamper around like puppies. In some versions, she's gentle. But in my head, she's snarky, because us young folk really are stupid sometimes. I looked forward to an age when I had all the answers.

Hopefully, I'd ask deeper questions than, "What the hell's a hot flash?"

But, one step at a time. My journey towards wisdom began when I was out shopping, for yarn of all things. Yarn—that domain of elderly women crocheting afghans, as well as hipster punk knitters making arm bands with fingerless gloves. "Which was I?" I thought as an onslaught of heat and dizziness forced me to sit down on a display of scrapbooking supplies.

It turns out that a hot flash is aptly named. It's heat flashing on you—sudden, intense, and unwelcome. I don't know why I was surprised.

I couldn't ask my mother if what I felt was normal. She hadn't hit menopause yet. My friends obviously had no clue. And my doctors were all men. They had told me what to expect, but couldn't give me the exact reassurances I was looking for. Mainly the answer to, "Do you really get this hot? For real? No…"

I knew what I had to do.

It was awkward at first, chiming into a new watercooler conversation at work. Boy did I get a look when I tried to commiserate with the lot of menopausal goddesses. For a brief, terrifying second, I thought they were about to unleash the full power of the pantheon and smite me. Knitted arm bands wouldn't save me. They thought this puppy was mocking them. I almost weed myself.

But, being wise, they figured it out. Lupron and Tamoxifen were drugs that forced some of us into goddess mode fully unprepared.

Yes, they told me, it really does get that hot. It is that sudden, and sometimes you get so dizzy that you do need to take a seat in the middle of the scrapbooking supplies. But that's okay, because a goddess can take a seat wherever she likes.

The Fifth Annual "Leena's Not Dead Party"
1 ½ Minutes

It was very right.

Well, okay, maybe a few people thought it was kind of wrong. But I liked it. It's not every day your mom hangs a homemade banner from the trees that says, "The Fifth Annual Leena's Not Dead Party."

It was a good time. The party, I mean. And the not being dead. The cancer that put me in this situation in the first place—that was kind of wrong.

But hey, bygones are bygones, for the most part. I'm hanging out in the woods next to the beach with fifty or so of my closest friends and family. So what if I can't play some pick-up volleyball because the ball impact will make my arms swell up in some freaky cancer lymph node thing. I was never good at volleyball anyway. I'll just have a beer instead.

My new boyfriend is here. Isn't he cute? He's also smart, and brave too. He's meeting my family for the first time. No pressure. I'm sure lots of future husbands meet their future wives' family at a "Not Dead" party. But, just in case, don't tell him I said that. Just because he's "The One" doesn't mean we don't have a very important dating process to respect.

I'm trying to respect all the processes in my life actually, and appreciate that not everything needs to be perfect. I may not be positive of the outcome, but, things look pretty good. I've made it five years without a relapse. And my boyfriend doesn't seem to be scared away by an irreverent banner slogan.

So yeah, I'd say things are very right. They are just as they should be.

Young People and Breast Cancer

According to the American Cancer Society[1], about five percent of breast cancer cases in the United States occur in women under the age of 40.

Most of these cases occur when a young woman has a mutated BRCA1 or BRCA2 gene, or when a close genetic family member had breast cancer.

And then sometimes it just appears out of the blue anyway. That's what happened to me.

There's some validity to the claim that breast cancer in young women is more dangerous than breast cancer in older women. It often takes young women longer to be diagnosed, for a few different reasons. One, our breast

---

[1] American Cancer Society, Breast Cancer Facts & Figures 2009-2010

tissue is often dense, which makes it harder for both people and machines to find the lumps. Two, because the odds of the lump being cancerous are so low, we might be told to wait (for too long) to see if it goes away.

Young women also tend to have more aggressive breast cancer than their older counterparts. This could partially be attributed to waiting longer for the diagnosis. But young women are also more apt to have something called "triple-negative" breast cancer, which can be more aggressive and more likely to reoccur than other subtypes of breast cancer[2].

I was lucky because I found my lump while it was still small, and received quality medical care that took my issue seriously. I was also lucky that I was not a triple-negative patient.

---

[2] Triple Negative Breast Cancer Foundation Website, Understanding Triple-Negative Breast Cancer 2011

I state in the monologue "Him" that my breast hurt. This is not the case for many women. Everyone has a different experience. Please know the risk factors, do self-exams to know your own breasts, and have a clinical breast exam every three years. Here are some breast changes to watch out for[3]:

- Lump, hard knot or thickening
- Swelling, warmth, redness or darkening
- Change in the size or shape of the breast
- Dimpling or puckering of the skin
- Itchy, scaly sore or rash on the nipple
- Pulling in of your nipple or other breast parts
- Nipple discharge that starts suddenly
- New pain in one spot that doesn't go away

If your worst fears come true, and you do find a lump, please don't panic. Again, the odds of the lump being a

---

[3] Susan G. Komen for the Cure, Facts for Life: Young Women and Breast Cancer 2010

cancerous tumor are low. But if it is cancer, know that it's a very treatable cancer. Eighty-nine percent of those treated for breast cancer will survive five years, and 82 percent will survive 10 years[4].

If you perform self-exams, get your breast checked by a professional every few years, and call a doctor the second something is out of the ordinary, you've done the best you could to help yourself and have maximized the odds of surviving and thriving. Trust me. Knowing that you've done all you could do makes a huge difference in getting through the worst-case scenario.

---

[4] American Cancer Society. Breast Cancer Facts & Figures 2009-2010, 2009

Author Assessments

There are pages for performance notes in the back of this book. These are for recording your own thoughts and ideas.

If you seek more insight into a piece, an author assessment of each monologue is available at leenaluther.com.

You can also record and upload your performances to the web for critiques and feedback.

YouTube: youtube.com/user/lumplogues
Vimeo: vimeo.com/groups/lumplogues

Performance Rights

These monologues may be used for auditioning purposes, monologue contests, and academic assessment. Inquiries into further rights may be directed to query@sublimitypress.com.

Acknowledgements

This collection wouldn't have been written without the following people. Thank you so much for your support.

Susan Albarran
Jennifer Boucher Albers
Kathy Carey Bagnoli
June Bischoff
Stephanie Biggs
Michael and Patricia Carey
Nancy Chamberlain
Jaimie Oliver Dill
Sandra Durante
Megan Giammatteo
Michael Graf
Emilee Greenhouse
Holly Griesser
Lisa Henderson
Hank Henkel
Phillip Katz
Stephanie Kennett
Laurie Maddalena
Tiffany Mathews
Emilie Nangle
Michelle Secor
Nicole Sfara-Casey
Dan and Sarah Strzelec
Cheryl Szczepkowski
Kerrie Wolf

Giving Back

A percentage of proceeds from book will go to cancer charities. Visit leenaluther.com to learn which charity will benefit each month.

Performance Notes
Him

Performance Notes
I Love New York

Performance Notes
Skeptical Looks

Performance Notes
The Princess with the Pea

Performance Notes

Odds Are

Performance Notes
Checking Out the Goods in the Chemo Room

Performance Notes
Soap Opera Fantasy Land

Performance Notes
Why Bloodhounds Look So Sad

Performance Notes
Whipping Off the Wig

Performance Notes
Chemo Dreams

Performance Notes
The Power of Puff

Performance Notes
My Orange Tic Tac

Performance Notes
Mistaken Identity

Performance Notes
My Cat Plays the Harp, and Other Non Sequiturs

Performance Notes
Scars

Performance Notes
Dress Code

Performance Notes
The Fourth State of Matter

Performance Notes
The Crone Goddess-in-Training Definition of a Hot Flash

Performance Notes
The Fifth Annual "Leena's Not Dead" Party

www.ingramcontent.com/pod-product-compliance
Lightning Source LLC
Chambersburg PA
CBHW020008050426
42450CB00005B/369